MESSAGES I NEVER SENT!

KUNAL RAJANI

Presentation by *BookLeaf Publishing*

Web: www.bookleafpub.com

E-mail: info@bookleafpub.com

ISBN: 9789357741378

First edition 2023

*This is for you my baby girl, I call you MBA
but could never really express how it meant
MY BEAUTIFUL ALCHEMIST, someone
who turned a nickel like me into gold.*

ACKNOWLEDGEMENT

I would like to acknowledge all my readers of my past books soul candy and sunflowers on the horizon as well as all the people reading this book right now, you readers and your feedback is what has helped me gain enough will power to write all these years.

PREFACE

this book is my way of expressing my one sided love for a special someone who doesn't even know it and maybe she never will, I am after all too much of a scared cat to man up and say it out loud but maybe this book will do the trick and if any of you got some suggestions or feedback regarding both my love life and this book do not hesitate to drop a text.... @ar.rk_

THE JEALOUS SKIES

The skies are holding me tight,
They can feel my loneliness,
They know I miss you tonight,
Without you I am always something less.

But fear not my heart says,
Also agrees the moon,
When its time for sunrays,
I will see you again soon.

Once again under the sky that is blue,
Our paths as are destined will cross,
Because these feelings undefined are true,
In our destiny its a chance a coin toss.

When that time does come,
Neither of us will be able to run,
In the background will play a drum,
Sounding like a baarat shooting a gun.

In that moment when I hug you,
The time will stop almost disappear,
Because it will be something long overdue,
And everything like a glass will become clear.

All the doubts and worries fading away,
With each breath you and I take,
In that moment the sky will say,
Jealous of us colors it will make.

An aurora we might call it,
It will be the sky turning grey,
Together when we will sit,
Under the sky of warm may.

All the birds will stop chirping,
In the awe of birds never seen,
The ones that were flirting,
Without speaking just with a glean.

The nature will be astounded,
By a love unprecedented,
We will be surrounded,
By the flowers most scented.

All I ask is wait for that day,
For it may come never or sooner than you think,
When its the time for sunrays,
When we meet under the sky that's pink.

A LOVERS DILEMMA

I don't like it
When I cant see u
I feel like I am knit
In the sky that is blue

When the sky turns dark
My eyes look for you
You have left your mark
With a love that is true

The sky turns orange
And I know its dawn
This feeling is strange
To you I am drawn

Every night when I lose
I pray to an entity
And I call a truce
Just to see you back in city

My mind has been blown
Never knew its capabilities
To the wolves I have been thrown
Travelled across a million cities

In the hopes of seeing you in one
Where the sky turns blue
That is when I will be done
Right then a hug will be due
Because I will be knit once more to the sky that
is blue

LOVING IN THE SKIES!

5

Colour me the colour of sky When sun rises,
So that i can feel the bird chirping in me,
I am ready to pay all the prices,
To see this world beyond whats you and me.

Colour me the colour of sky when sun has risen,
So that i can bring warmth to the plants and
trees,
It would feel like i am being put in prison,
But i would do it so the world could see.

Colour me the colour of sky when sun starts to
descend,
So that everyone can feel rested in me,
That is when i feel i would start to ascend,
And from this existence i will be free.

Colour me the colour of sky when sun sets,
So that everyone may know its time to indulge,
So that everyone knows its time to forget the
regrets,
It would be a felony not to divulge.

Colour me the colour of sky when sun has set,

So in the darkness of the night everyone can
confess,
In the misery of others i might forget,
How miserable i was in that pretty dress.

But most importantly,
Colour me the colour of sky when it displays the
aurora,
So that i can become a beacon of hope,
That would make me one with the flora,
And i might forget i was at the end of the rope.

This is my hope and so are my dreams,
To see the world be better when i leave,
The world was a cruel place it seems,
But i made it a little better with my grieve,
And i was still remembered when i became a has
been.

A LETTER NEVER SENT!

Today will be powerful,
As powerful as a Sun,
The noises will be earful,
But soothing like a Drum.

This day is a gift for you,
From someone with love,
Since the intentions are true,
The commands and wishes are from above.

Believe in yourself my love,
As you ask me to do everyday,
I am sending your way a dove,
That will keep the problems at bay.

You say you are not mine,
And yet the bond is the same,
Every time together we dine,
And I crack a joke that's lame.

You find laughter in it,
For you care so very much,
To not let me feel I don't fit,
You are a princess Dutch.

I hope from the bottom of my heart,
Every time you read this poem you laugh,
For this poem is both my love and my art,
But every time you do don't feel apart,
For I am always watching over you since I am as
tall as a giraffe.

BOTH HAPPY AND SAD
WHEN I HELD YOU

Happy that I was near you,
Sad that you weren't mine,
Looking at a sky thats blue,
Feeling like trapped in a mine

Knowing that I had your trust,
It was all I had going,
Doing whatever I must,
To keep the wind blowing.

Bowing down my hat,
In my heart is nothing but you,
How do I say that?
Something thats long overdue...

Knowing that I loved you,
You couldnt say it right?
You weren't ready for something new,
Maybe its my fault I didn't fight....

But tonight under the stars,
All I want is you,
I have fought a lot of wars,
To be able to see the sky blue

The moon in its infinite wisdom,
Showed me the path to you,
The songs I hum,
Might have been a clue.

I have loved you with my breath dying,
I swear to the one you know,
And I wasn't lying,
When I said I am not letting go.

Spread your arms to welcome a hug,
Take a step to my humble throne,
Let me lie in the hole I dug,
Just don't leave me alone.

WHAT IS LOVE?

What is love?
Is the question I ask,
Is it a dove,
Or devil in a mask?

Love is pure,
That is what I had heard,
It is a cure,
But also it hurts.

I am on a path,
To find that love,
Will it bring Wrath,
When push comes to shove?

Will I find it?
Beautiful and pure,
Will I take a hit,
Or can it be a cure?

If I find the one,
The one I desire.
Am I gonna run?
Or jump into the fire?

When I find it,
Will I be strong?
Will I even fit?
Or even belong?

To answer it all,
I closed my eyes,
I broke a wall,
And found my life in your disguise.

WHY NOT?

Why not love like we used to?
Why not meet like we used to?
Why not frown like we used to?
Why not smile like we used to?

Why were we so close?
Why was your love such a high dose?
Why did we entwine our toes?
Why did I love the ring on your nose?

Why don't we talk anymore?
Why is it we don't connect no more?
Why do I remember last night what you wore?
Why am I now scared to knock on your door?

Why is it that we talk but we really don't?
Why is it that we don't know what we really
want?
Why do I run back to you no matter what?
Why can't I just let go?

I know the answer why?
I know you are in my heart,
Yet why does it make me cry?
Why did our ways part?

STORY OF MY LIFE!

I had you, didn't I?
Story of my life!
You wanted me then, didn't you?
Story of my life!

I neglected you, didn't I?
Story of my life!
I didn't fight hard enough, did I?
Story of my life!

I fooled around thinking you wouldn't leave,
didn't I?
Story of my life!
I should have paid more attention I didn't, did I?
Story of my life!

Yet you loved me with all your heart, didn't you?
Not the story of my life!
You turned a brass man into Gold, didn't you?
Not the story of my life!

I should have cared more I didn't, did I?
Story of my life!
I should have fought harder I didn't, did I?
Story of my life!

And the story of my life turned into a tale,
To be regretted for life,
Maybe to you this letter I could mail,
Maye then you could be my wife.

Who am I?

Who am I who is the question I ask,
Am i product on sale in DMart?
Am I a job wearing a mask?
Who am I trying to outsmart?

Who am I is the question that remains,
Am i just a degree hanging in the frame?
Or am I a seat empty in the rains?
Is this my life or just a game ?

Another morning with same questions,
Who am I but no answers,
In the moment, I found my redemption,
Who am I if not my creations?

MY DAY

I wake up every morning,
Thinking its my first,
I sleep every night,
Thinking its my last.

Every hour of the day,
As it passes is my past,
Every hour of the day,
As it comes may be last.

Every night when I sleep,
I wonder if I will last,
The slope is very steep,
My heart may just blast.

And then again I wake up,
Every morning with a smile,
The sun rises too,
Away a thousand miles.

Our eyes cross paths,
The time slows,
It's not the first time,
And she knows.

Any tomorrow again,
We both know,
She will be crossing the street,
And I will be on my window.

A LIE?

In a web of lies,
A golden truth,
He lives like spies,
Even in his youth.

Every man is just a liar,
All sell lies,
Is what you said,
But is there a buyer?

A lie is hired,
Truth set free,
Can I even admire,
What I see?

The questions are infinite,
Answers none,
The questions are dynamite,
Answers, silent as a nun.

The lie ranges,
From old age to youth,
A lie changes,
Not the truth.

THE NIGHTS THAT WRITE

Every night,
When the sky is dark,
I pickup my pen
And on a journey I embark.

A journey of truth,
The path unknown,
It may steal my youth,
I might need a loan.

And yet every night,
I do it again,
My heart full of fright,
I say amen.

I am a commander,
A soldier of truth,
I speak with candor,
I even lost a tooth.

People abhor me,
Call me a misfit,
They cant agree,
That it is a gift.

A real gift,
To all mankind,
Everyone who was adrift,
Is now defined.

WONDERING EVERY NIGHT

On the crossroads of life,
Before a chance to drive,
I am standing with a knife,
Riddled with moral strife.

Asking where I went wrong?
What was my crime?
Everyday singing a new song,
Trying to count a new rhyme.

My life misled me,
Took me to a hive,
I was not a bee,
As a misfit I cried.

A LOVE LETTER

I am writing a letter to the woman I love,
Very old school is what she prefers,
If we were birds, she would be a dove,
Beautiful and tender, with unique feathers.

This letter is my confession to her,
Of all my love and respect for her,
And yet tomorrow I wont be able to post it,
Because I died a little the instance I wrote it.

The missing reply

My question is constant ur reply missing,
My question is constant ur reply missing,
The miss I know is slightly tipping,
She is a bit scared a bit confused,
Wat to do in a hurry amused?

U know me like there is no one around,
trust me I can take you to the crown,
Just trust and take a leap of faith,
for I am here with a tiara for your face.

MY LIGHT

I gave you my heart,
I gave you my soul,
You knew it from the start,
Only you could make me whole.

I loved you since the beginning,
And since then I have been begging,
And I really don't wish to be nagging,
But is this really the ending?

I love the way sun brightens up your face,
In that moment the whole universe fades away,
With eyes I flirt when meets our gaze,
And it surely always makes my day.

Seeing you in the morning,
Gives me a sense of hope,
Even when I am drowning,
It doesn't feel like the end of rope.

At the end of the night,
Is this a magical spell my love?
Knowing i can fight,
How do i always dream of a dove?

Is it you in my dreams,
Knocking every night?
Calling you in my screams,
Are you in the darkness my light?

IS IT RIGHT?

Is it right that I want you?
Because I really have loved you,
Is it right the way it feels?
Because I really dont know another way to.

I have loved you,
Ever since I laid my eyes on you,
Are these feelings really true,
Honestly I don't have a clue.

Under the starry skies,
In the darkness of this night,
Reading the lord of flies,
What we have seems right.

In a world of black and white,
Maybe we dont belong together,
But for you I can still fight,
Any tornado I can whither.

In this world of grey,
Maybe we have a shot,
In the sun's ray,
Under the moonlight in a yacht.

If I ask you if you love me,
Even if you can't be with me,
Would you say I do?
Would you stay till the sky turned blue?

WANTING YOU!

Kaafi shabd likh chuke
Aaj sacch batane ki baari hai
Kaise batau tujhe
tu mujhe kitni pyaari hai

Alfaazo ki gehraiyon mein
Bhavnao se na mukar jana
In shabdo ke jaalo mein
Is wakt se yuhi na guzar jaana

Kehne ko toh kai raaz hai
Pata nai kaise batana
Par mujhe tumse pyaar hai
Isse bhi kaise chupana

Jaanta hu kabhi dekha nahi
Mera hadd se guzar jaana
Maanta hu kabhi mila nai
Tumse us tarah dubara

Aaj b mein sochta hu
Kaise kar raha tha guzara
Jab tum nahi the mere pass
Aur naa hi koi sahara

Darta hu tumhe khone se
Kehta hu aaj fir dubara
Tumse door jaakar
Na fir hoga mera guzara

Roz kehta hu khudse
ban jaa patthar dil
Fir nai hoga yeh pyaar dobara
Par darta hu dil todne se
Mein b toh tha ek aashiq aawara

Jaanta hu kya bolegi
Meri yeh kavita sun
Chup karke rolunga
Gaakar fir ek nayi dhun

Jaanta hu bht pareshaan kiya hai
Is janam mein shayad naa milu dobara
Par pyaar bhi utna hi karta hu
Kya kehne ka yeh haqq hai humara

Jaanta hu tu darti hai
Par kya karu meri chahat ka
Tu hi toh kehti hai
Zaroorat nai chahat ka hu maara

Is fitrat ko badaldu mein
Modd du apni zaroorato ko
Par khwahisho ka kya karu

Kya kahu is matlab ko

I could change my nature
The very fabric of my life
I could change my needs
Even if I had to cut it with a knife

What I do not understand
my darling sweetheart
How do I change my wants
When I know you are the one!!!!

INSANE LOVE

Is this night or is this day?
Why am I not sure?
Am I dreaming in sun's ray?
Is this the cure?

Drowning in the ocean bay?
Weren't my intentions pure?
Is this the bed that I lay?
This task isn't foolish I am sure?
Like finding a needle in a stack of hay?

Give me a sign of wisdom universe!
I need to know I am not insane!
Asking for clarity in every verse!
Checking every second if I am in the right lane!

I know you will be mine one morning!
Knowing that is keeping me sane!
The sun is here again on me dawning!
Giving me a reality check in vain!

Ignore me all you want,
My love doesn't waive,
These nightmares do haunt,
But I never ever cave.

Fighting through the demons of night,
All my insecurities in place,
I persevere to the light,
Just once more to meet your gaze.

The one that makes me weak,
Weaker than a tender petal,
I climbed the mountain peak,
And now I couldn't settle.

For now I can see you in my arms
without a hint of doubt on a morning precious
with a hue in your eyes that would make the
angels scatter
and this is what I fought for with all my candor.

THE FIRST GLANCE

My heart was captured when I saw you in that
white top
With those big round earrings that just flopped
You stole my heart in that moment can I call a
cop?
In the joy that I found you just like a bunny I
hopped.

In the sins of my past I looked down upon
myself
Its ok Kunal you are just a human it happens you
said
It was like I was a fallen antique put back on the
glorious shelf
In the happiness of that moment my heart just
bled

You looked into my soul to find the man I once
was
Turned me into a human being with desires once
more
To protect me from your eyes blazing into my
soul should be some laws
I cant believe how I was alive or even if I was
before?

You came into my life and my heart skipped a
beat
Its like you are my other half that was missing
from me
You pulled the earth underneath me before I
could take a seat
And since then before you I have always taken a
knee

I admire you because you inspire me
I adore you because you are my destiny
How do I hide on my face the glee?
Every time you look back I hear a melody ♫

In your soul I have found my redemption
In your face I see my distinction
In my heart is a clear dysfunction
For you say its crowded but only you have its
attention

My poor little heart weeps and weeps
It cries aloud even when I sleep
Around your mention it skips its beeps
That is how buried you are in deep

After all is said and done the morning will sing a
song different
You know I have always loved and always I will

I have given you a lot of clues even numerous
hint
For you my baby girl I wont hesitate to kill

You may think I am the hero
But I portray not my identity
I am the true villain
Who calculates the intensity

For you my love the world is a matchstick
Without a second thought I will burn it
All my wounds everyday I lick
And I will shred it to a bit

I am crossing the lines every night
To see you in the morning lit
I will fall from the height
And a homerun I will hit

Name your desires my alchemist
Your wishes are my commands
All the people around are mist
I wish to walk with you in the sands

I will never let you go is what I said
I will be by your side is what I meant
If I had even a little bit of head
I would have never fallen for your scent

But I am addicted now
In love with your kiss
Everyday I just bow
And every moment I miss

Survive I will how?
How will I find this bliss?
In the sanctuary of my heart
Lies a place for you still…………

FAREWELL ARTIST!

Everyday I wake up with a dream
Every night I cry when it breaks
Every day is new it seems
But every night is the same

I have a lot to say but not a lot of ways
I have a lot to do but not a lot of days
My ship wants to be anchored
But I don't have a bay

Every tear I shed I hope is my last
Every year I say this time it will last
Every day I wake up I hope is my last
Every night I sleep this time might be last

Around the world I travelled
On a journey I embarked
Saw a lot of things
That made me who we are

Every time I look out the windows
I see a sky full of stars
Every morning i see the sun
And yet also the stars

Am I going crazy or is it just my heart?
I thought I was ready but not my heart
Every night I ask myself is it okay to last?
To have nothing to cherish and still just go fast?

I am running in a race
Not sure who I am trying to outsmart
Am I running in a maze?
Maybe this is my last

I thought I knew everything
Maybe I learned something new
I thought I had seen all the colors
But I had never seen this hue

The moon taunts me tonight
Asks me where are you?
My lips are sealed tight
Waiting for the sky to turn blue

My eyes all watery
My dreams almost broken
My motives all void
My life almost over

Lying in this bed
Everything seems untrue
Where was I led?
Where is my crew?

All the people I relied on
Everyone I thought true
All of them turned their backs
To my pains in the times when due

Consider this my last poem
Under the night of stars
I have fallen and fallen
But cant get up behind bars

This is a farewell to the artist inside me
This is my carol to the feelings to be
I cant write anymore to say the things I cant
I cant take it anymore to stay and rant